M*MMY CUSSES

INSPIRING PROFANITY AND STIMULATING SARCASM FOR MAMAS WHO'VE SEEN IT ALL

BY SERENA DORMAN ∨ ILLUSTRATED BY PAIGE VICKERS

CHRONICLE BOOKS
SAN FRANCISCO

Text copyright © 2021 by Serena Dorman.
Illustrations copyright © 2021 by Paige Vickers.
All rights reserved. No part of this book may be reproduced in any form without written permission from the publisher.

Library of Congress Cataloging-in-Publication Data

Names: Dorman, Serena, author.
Title: Mommy cusses : inspiring profanity and stimulating sarcasm for moms who have seen it all / by Serena Dorman.
Description: San Francisco : Chronicle Books, [2021]
Identifiers: LCCN 2020017207 | ISBN 9781797204123 (hardcover) | ISBN 9781797206240 (ebook)
Subjects: LCSH: Mothers—United States—Humor. | Motherhood—United States—Humor.
Classification: LCC PN6231.M68 D67 2021 | DDC 818/.602—dc23
LC record available at https://lccn.loc.gov/2020017207

Manufactured in China.
Design by Rachel Harrell.
10 9 8 7 6 5 4 3 2

MIX
Paper from responsible sources
FSC® C008047

Chronicle books and gifts are available at special quantity discounts to corporations, professional associations, literacy programs, and other organizations. For details and discount information, please contact our premiums department at corporatesales@chroniclebooks.com or at 1-800-759-0190.

Chronicle Books LLC
680 Second Street
San Francisco, California 94107
www.chroniclebooks.com

Bill Nye the Science Guy is a registered trademark of Bill Nye, As Trustee of the Revocable Living Trust of Bill Nye; Blue's Clues is a registered trademark of Viacom International Inc; Caillou is a registered trademark of Chouette Publishing Inc.; Captain Planet is a registered trademark of TBS Productions, Inc; Casper the Friendly Ghost is a registered trademark of Classic Media, LLC; Crown Royal is a registered trademark of Diageo North America, Inc.; Disney princess is a registered trademark of Disney Enterprises, Inc.; Edward Scissorhands is a registered trademark of Twentieth Century Fox Film Corporation; Facebook is a registered trademark of Facebook, Inc.; Goofy is a registered trademark of Disney Enterprises, Inc.; Hulk is a registered trademark of Marvel Characters, Inc; Kidz Bop is a registered trademark of Kidz Bop Enterprises LLC; Lego is a registered trademark of Lego Juris A/S Corporation; MacGyver is a registered trademark of Auras Unlimited Productions, Inc.; Magic 8 Ball is a registered trademark of Mattel, Inc.; Megamind is a registered trademark of DreamWorks Animation L.L.C.; Mister Rogers is a registered trademark of Mcfeely-Rogers Foundation; Mockingjay is a registered trademark of District 12, LLC; Mr. Bean is a registered trademark of Tiger Aspect Productions; Mr. Clean is a registered trademark of The Procter & Gamble Company; Netflix is a registered trademark of Netflix, Inc.; Pee-Wee Herman is a registered trademark of Paul Reubens; Pepto Bismol is a registered trademark of The Procter & Gamble Company; Pinterest is a registered trademark of Pinterest, Inc.; Polaroid is a registered trademark of PLR IP Holdings, LLC; Pop-Tarts is a registered trademark of Kellogg North America Company; Power Rangers is a registered trademark of SCG Power Rangers LLC; Sanctimommy is a registered trademark of Grace Hussar; Scooby-Doo is a registered trademark of Hanna-Barbera Productions, Inc; Sleep Number is a registered trademark of Sleep Number Corporation; Snoopy is a registered trademark of Peanuts Worldwide LLC; Target is a registered trademark of Target Brands, Inc; Tarzan is a registered trademark of Edgar Rice Burroughs, Inc.; Teletubbies is a registered trademark of Ragdoll Worldwide Ltd; Tetris is a registered trademark of Tetris Holding, LLC; The Wiggles is a registered trademark of Wiggles Pty Limited; Toys "R" Us is a registered trademark of Tru Kids Inc.; Twenty Questions is a registered trademark of University Games Corporation; WD-40 is a registered trademark of WD-40 Manufacturing Company; Wreck-It Ralph is a registered trademark of Disney Enterprises, Inc.; WWE is a registered trademark World Wrestling Entertainment, Inc.; Xena is a registered trademark of NBCUniversal Media, LLC; Zootopia is a registered trademark of Disney Enterprises, Inc.

For my husband, son, and daughter.

"No other soul could love
you like my rotten bones do."

—*The Gaslight Anthem*

CONTENTS

Introduction: Dear Fellow Snack Bitch 8

WTF 12

Periodic Table of Essentials for Moms 15

Alternate Titles for This Book 16

How to Look Like You Have Your Shit Together 18

Hey Girl, Wanna Be My Mom Friend? 21

M.A.S.H. for Moms 22

What Childbirth Feels Like 27

Insult Generator for Unsolicited Parenting Advice 30

Welcome to Life as Someone's Nap Slut 32

Your Day as a Parent According to Your Astrological Sign 34

To the Mom Sitting in the Dark 38

The Kudos We All Deserve 40

How to Mom-Proof Your Home 43

How to Co-Sleep in 2,457 Easy Steps 47

Marry, Screw, Kill for Parents 52

Five Yoga Poses for Dealing with Your Child's Bullshit 56

Rap Names for Kids 60

Tactical Hand Signals for Parents 62

To the Mom I Wanted to Be 64

What Kind of Mom Are You? 69

Sex Positions for Parents 76

Tactics for Exiting a Sleeping Child's Room 79

Things Parents Can Add to Their Résumé 83

A Timeline of Going Anywhere with Kids 85

How to (Not) Get Your Child into a Car Seat 88

Sorry I'm Late (A Tardy Slip for Parents) 90

How to Calm Your Tits 92

11 Rules for Playdating My Child 96

Magic 8-Ball for Moms 98

When Kids Cry: Very Sciencey Statistics 101

How to Pee if You're a Boy 102

Am I a Good Parent? Quiz 106

Afterword 110

Acknowledgments 112

DEAR FELLOW SNACK BITCH,

You're wearing more bodily fluids than a porn star, the sink is full of dishes, and the floor is covered in toys, crumbs, clean laundry you have no energy to fold, and abandoned goals for the day. The kids are in bed but Mom Guilt keeps you wide awake. The couch dips as Mom Guilt sits next to you and breathes worry and frustration into your soul so thick and black that you can't see all the ways you glittered today.

There's an itch at the bottom of your soul that you can't seem to scratch, and you ache to hear another parent say, "I'm struggling too." Not because you want someone else to feel like a failure, but because you want to feel a little less alone, a little less crazy. That you're not imagining how incredibly hard being a parent can be.

This is motherhood. It's a dream, it's a mess, it's beautiful, and it's everything in between. It's dipping from one polar extreme to the other, sometimes within minutes. It's a love deeper than anything you've ever known, and a grief that's more agonizing too. It's holding your child long after they've fallen asleep to beg them for forgiveness. It's late nights giggling together and making memories, and then it's realizing that sometimes you're the monster hiding beneath your child's bed.

HOME IS WHERE THE KIDS ARE CRYING & FUCKING SHIT UP

In case no one has told you lately and you're starting to forget, you're pretty fucking amazing. Read that again, and let yourself believe it for once. We're all just grasping at straws, trying to make a little sense of this shitastrophe.

So, when motherhood starts to punt you in the puss and you start thinking you're alone, know that even though you can't see us, you have an invisible army of perfectly imperfect moms in your corner. You've got this.

Mommy Cusses is a wildly inappropriate book full of snark, sarcasm, and swears that offers a variety of uninspirational quotes, momtivities, and general malarkey to entertain you. Flip to a page, any page, and find a hilarious escape from that load of laundry or those dishes you don't want to do anyway. There's no need to read from cover to cover because, let's face it, you're a parent and parents don't have time for such leisurely pleasures.

Things you can do with this book:

- Use it as a partition when someone tries to make small talk, give you unsolicited parenting advice, or sell you essential oils.

- Swat at fingers under the bathroom door with it while you're trying to enjoy an unrushed shit for once.

- Set it on your baby's head to read while nursing.

- Use it as a sneeze guard to keep your acquaintance from high school's spittle from landing on your lip again as she salivates at the thought of adding you to her multilevel marketing team.

- Eat snacks behind it.

- Close it dramatically in the midst of an argument.

- Cover your nipples with it the next time someone shows up at your door unannounced and you didn't have time to put on a bra.

- Peek at people awkwardly over the top of it after denying that the kid throwing a tantrum is yours despite the fact that they keep yelling, "Stop, Mommy!" every time you ask where their mother is.

- Carry it around so people think you are an adulty adult who, like, reads and stuff.

- Enjoy!

WTF

Motherhood is just a series of WTF moments: What the fuck? Where the fuck? Who the fuck and why the fuck?

There are three truths to parenting:

- You never know more about how to raise a child than before you actually have one.

- No one knows WTF they're doing. Nope, not even Janet on Facebook with her endless photos of wholesome meals and a dining room table that actually serves as a dining room table instead of a platform for clean laundry.

- Children delight in creating new and exciting ways to mindfuck you into oblivion every day.

To the mom with a shaky smile, staring longingly at the bottle of Moscato in the wine aisle as her child writhes on the floor, screaming that they want Pop-Tarts. To the parent who thinks they are failing in comparison to everyone else because Sally's kid knows Mandarin, or Timmy's mom makes gluten-free, glittery, multicolored, unicorn-fart-scented spaghetti zoodles: I salute you.

Nurse (handing me a newborn):
You got this?

Me: Sometimes I have to dig through the trash to reread the instructions for mac 'n' cheese; so no, I don't got this.

Parenting is a lot like that party game where they blindfold you, spin you around, guide you in a general direction, and laugh.

PERIODIC TABLE OF ESSENTIALS FOR MOMS

S — one million selfies of your child in your camera roll that they took of themselves

TO — smells like takeout for dinner

SS — stress sweat, because you and your kid are playing tug-o-war with the restroom lock

C — concealer

DS — dry shampoo

T — trash tv

MB — messy bun

DC — dark circles and 2 years of sleep debt

2pac — Kidz Bop on the way to school, '90s rap on the way home

MD — murder docs

C — coffee

PC — phone charger

B — booze

I — ibuprofen

SP — smartphone

EW — elastic waistband

BL — black leggings, a pair (or five) for home and a dressy pair

WW — wet wipes, to use on anything and everything

OS — oversize shirt

S — sunglasses, to hide the fact that you're mostly dead inside

SL — shirtsleeve with your kid's trail of snot

ALTERNATE TITLES FOR THIS BOOK

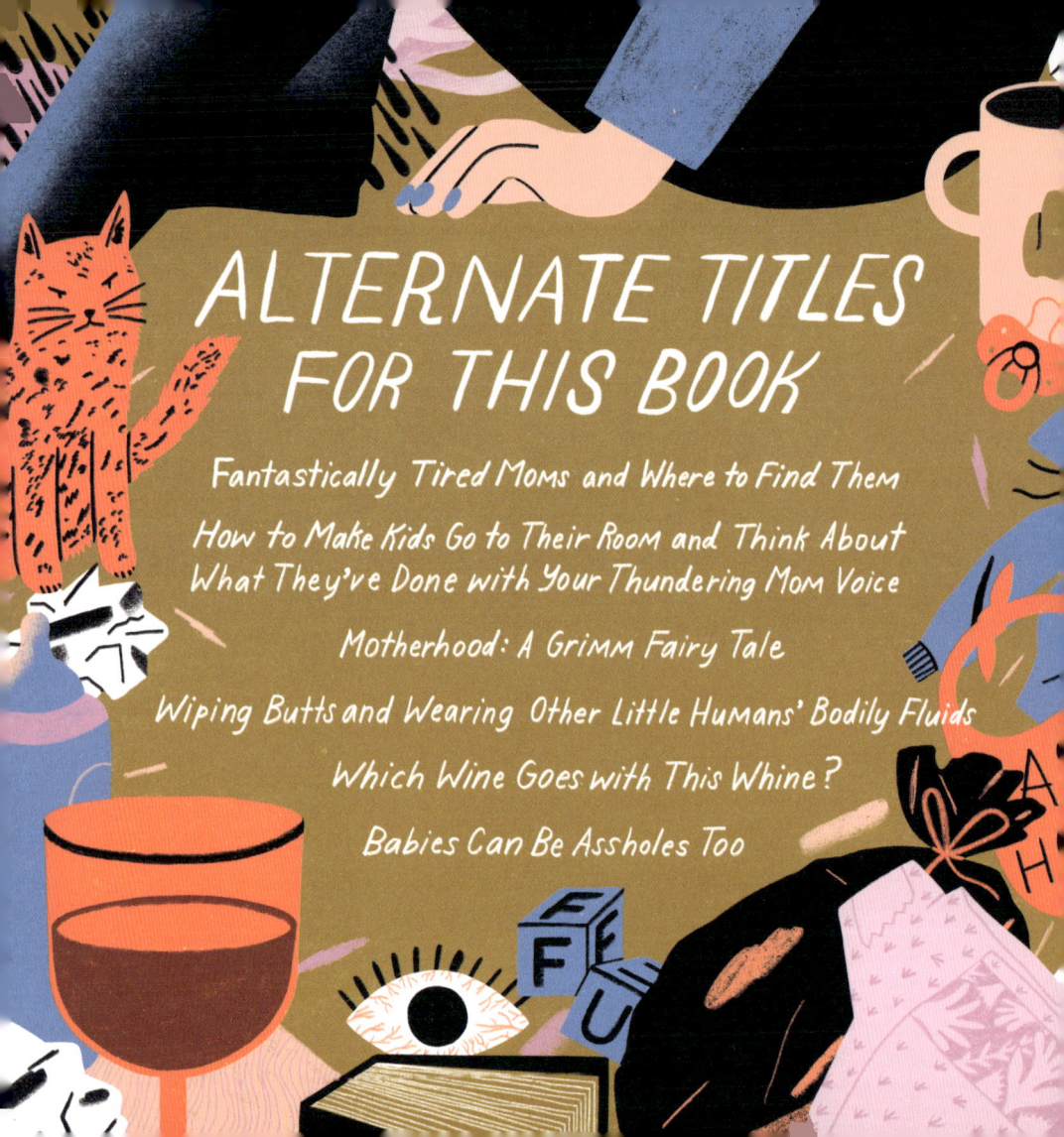

Fantastically Tired Moms and Where to Find Them

How to Make Kids Go to Their Room and Think About What They've Done with Your Thundering Mom Voice

Motherhood: A Grimm Fairy Tale

Wiping Butts and Wearing Other Little Humans' Bodily Fluids

Which Wine Goes with This Whine?

Babies Can Be Assholes Too

How to summon a mom: Make a circle with black leggings, play some '90s rap, put a Target bull's-eye in the center, and start making margaritas.

HOW TO LOOK LIKE YOU HAVE YOUR SHIT TOGETHER

Most of us fully intended, once we became mothers, to be one of those nicely dressed, organized, bento box–wielding sorceresses we see on social media. Somewhere along the way, we managed to stumble onto the Hot Mess Express with a one-way ticket to the Shit Show.

From one hot mess mom to another, here are a few tips on how to look like a total pro at this whole mom thing.

- When someone asks if you want to do something, say you need to check your schedule. Which is code for, "I never know what day it is, and even if I did, there's no way I'd get it together to leave the house on time."

- Buy some cardigans. Moms who have their shit together love cardigans. It's science.

- Keep a fancy pen on your person and whip it out whenever you have to sign anything, even if a pen is provided to you. Especially if another pen is provided to you.

- Keep your car clean. Even better, toss in an air freshener or douse the car with spray if you're carpooling. Make it smell like a hula girl drinking piña coladas out of coconuts is stuffed in the trunk.

- Listen to the news just long enough to hear something interesting, and then repeat it to anyone who will listen. Current events are current and eventful.

- Take up a fancy hobby, like black-and-white photography of doll shoes or something else very weird and specific. People will think you have time to be unique.

- Keep pretty little packages of tissues on you so you can swoop in to wipe orifices on your child's face or offer one to another parent in need. Like some kind of majestic ninja snot fairy.

- If people are visiting your home, make sure to stage an educational kid's activity that you "haven't had time to clean up." What to say: "Oh, that? We were just experimenting with phosphorescent compounds by combining various polyvinyl alcohol solutions and borate ions." What it means: We made glow-in-the-dark slime.

Congratulations! You have successfully tricked people into believing you're not a train wreck. Now go drink straight from the nozzle of your boxed wine. You've earned it.

You doing 18 years to life too?
—Me, trying to make mom friends at the playground

HEY GIRL, WANNA BE MY MOM FRIEND?

Hello! My name is _____. I'd love to get together sometime for a mom playdate. I'm writing because (check all that apply):

- [ ] I tried to make conversation but I'm socially awkward.
- [ ] I am the owner of tiny humans who make adult interaction impossible.
- [ ] I was rage-walking out the door with my kid under an arm like a surfboard because they were throwing a tantrum.
- [ ] I was in a rush because I'm a mom and therefore perpetually late to everything at all times.
- [ ] I didn't anticipate getting out of the car and was dressed in my pajamas.
- [ ] I creepily eavesdropped on a conversation you were having and think we could be best friends.
- [ ] Your cart (filled with wine, ice cream, and a DIY slime kit) and my cart (filled with new black leggings sans crotch holes, a kid's movie, and a year's supply of coffee) seem like soulmates.

We could (check all that apply):

- [ ] Bake shit
- [ ] Watch murder documentaries
- [ ] Have a kitchen dance party to '90s hip-hop
- [ ] Day drink
- [ ] Stuff our faces
- [ ] Get manis/pedis/brazillians while we hold hands
- [ ] Let our kids play while we eat their good snacks

My number is _____.

M*A*S*H

Instructions:

1. Fill out the questions below on a separate piece of paper.
2. Draw a circle, and inside of that circle, draw a spiral.
3. Draw a line through the center of the spiral and draw a dot wherever the center line intersects with the rings of your spiral.
4. Count the dots. This will be your magical number.
5. In each category (starting with the M.A.S.H. title), count through each answer until you reach your magical number (you may have to go through your list more than once), and then cross that answer out. Continue to count and cross out answers until you're left with only one. That will be your M.A.S.H. result!

Age you'll become a grandma

1. When my daughter is 50
2. When I'm retired and achieving my dream of floating down a lazy river while drinking wine out of a Pringles can
3. I already have the soul and energy of a much more geriatric person
4. Before dementia sets in, so I can delight in my grandkids dishing out some karma

Celebrity mom crush who will become your BFF

1. Ali Wong
2. Chrissy Teigen
3. Amy Schumer
4. Nicole Richie

What you'll do on your next solo outing

1. What is a solo outing?
2. Buy a phony passport and fake my own death
3. Take my sweet-ass time roaming the aisles of my favorite store
4. Unhinge my jaw and eat junk food I don't have to share in my car with my music on full blast

Date you'll have with your mom friends

1. Hahahahaha—that would require free time
2. Day drinking and talking shit
3. A staycation in a hotel room where I can order room service and not have to clean up after anyone
4. A grown-ass-women sleepover with snacks and rom-coms, but we're all in bed by 10 p.m.

Number of times you'll lose your shit today

1. I lose my shit so much that my kids probably think their names are "SHIT!"
2. If you're reading this, it means I did not make it; tell the police my kids did this to me
3. I'm going strong at 5 l.s.p.h. (lost shits per hour)
4. DMX—which are the roman numerals for "Y'ull gon' make me lose my mind—up in here, up in here" (it's facts)

Drink you'll enjoy after the kids go to bed

1. Embalming fluid, because my children won't sleep until I am dead
2. Coffee—while it's still hot!
3. Liquid melatonin, because I'm exhausted
4. Whiskey with a Pepto-Bismol chaser

The only floor in this house not covered in toys and crumbs is my pelvic floor.

Burglar (trying to break into my home/struggling with the baby gate): WTF!?

Me: It's a—you have to pull with your thumb while you LIFT.

Burglar: Like this? I don't—

Me: Yeah, yeah, now LIFT.

Burglar (jiggling gate): You know what? I'll try a different house. You have a good night!

My Son: You've been grumpy for like 2 years.

Me: How old is your sister?

Son: 2.

Me: Weird.

WHAT CHILDBIRTH FEELS LIKE

Death by T-Rex bite to your lady garden

Being kicked in the crotch by a kangaroo on uppers

Going to third base with Edward Scissorhands

Lighting your lady bits on fire

Having hundreds of bees trapped inside your thong

Getting finger-blasted by jalapeños

Getting jackhammered by an actual jackhammer

Straddling Mount St. Helens

After kids, my body is no longer a wonderland. More like a rickety playground climbing structure in the shady part of town.

I'M MAKING A VAGINA-SHAPED PIÑATA FOR MY CHILD TO DESTROY ON THEIR BIRTHDAY— BECAUSE HISTORICAL ACCURACY IS IMPORTANT

INSULT GENERATOR FOR UNSOLICITED PARENTING ADVICE

hey	eat	someone's	shit
you should	guzzle	a trucker's	toilet scum
go	pound	copious amounts of	bellybutton lint
why don't you	cuddle	a wolverine's	buttholes
yo	suck	a bag of	pubes
	bathe in	some	teets
	lick	a vat of	farts
	snort	pounds of	piss
	suckle	your ex's	labes
	poke	a loaf of	afterbirth
	sit in	a liter of	prostates
	roll in	a truckload of	areolas
	chug	a clown's	dicks
	huff	bigfoot's	foreskin

Sometimes I think I'm a good parent. Until I see a parent-ier parent parenting all over the place.

WELCOME TO LIFE AS SOMEONE'S NAP SLUT

Salutations, fellow nap slut.

Every parent is a good little nap servant for their children. Some of us go to more extreme lengths, but peer in on any parent during nap time and you'll see all the bizarre stunts we're willing to pull just to lull our children into sweet unconsciousness . . . so we're free to procrastinate on the long list of responsible, adulty shit in exchange for a few hours of staring at our phones like slack-jawed Neanderthals while trash TV plays in the background.

Fun book trivia: I mentally wrote this as I lay with one arm elbow-deep through the slats of my daughter's crib while the sound machine subliminally called me a dickhead.

Every child has their own little secret sleep combination that they keep locked down tighter than Fort Knox. Their "Sleep Number" is zero, as in there's zero chance of you leaving their room with your sanity intact. But here are a few of the techniques you're likely to try anyway:

Army crawling out of their room	**Blood magic**
Singing	**Climbing in the crib with them**
Juggling knives	**Essential oils**
Playing dead	**Hypnosis**
Patting them on the back through the crib rails	**Shushing. Shushing harder. Harder, until you run out of air and pass out.**
Rocking, swaying, bouncing, or some absurd combination of the three that you'll find yourself doing even when your child isn't in your arms	**Bamboozling them by caressing them with a decapitated-arm prop and then leaving it in their crib**

Sleep experts make a killing writing books and selling products and e-courses that exhausted parents throw money at because we're desperate, but the truth is—we're all just fucked.

YOUR DAY AS A PARENT ACCORDING TO YOUR ASTROLOGICAL SIGN

Aries: Your kid will whine about a bump in their sock.

Libra: You will spend nap time scrolling on your phone instead of doing the 192 tasks you need to finish.

Cancer: A grocery store tantrum followed by your kid airing all your dirty laundry to the cashier is in your future.

Gemini: You made a wholesome, seven-course dinner. Your kid wanted pizza, so you compromised and ordered pizza.

Leo: Wearing pj's all day turns from sad and unproductive to festive and whimsical if you make it a theme.

Virgo: Your kid is having a meltdown because you poured their juice into the red cup with blue stripes instead of the blue cup with red stripes (it's the same damn cup!).

Aquarius: You will mutter: "For fuck's sake" at least twice and flip your kids off behind their backs at least five times.

Taurus: You will reheat your coffee in the microwave thrice.

Scorpio: You will scream at your kid at least twenty times to stop touching their penis/vagina.

Capricorn: It's gonna be a wine-in-your-coffee-cup-for-breakfast kind of day.

Sagittarius: You will read a helpful book (ahem) reminding you to switch your laundry from the washing machine to the dryer. You're welcome.

Pisces: You will spend 2 hours busting your ass over a dinner your kids will complain about until they're eighteen.

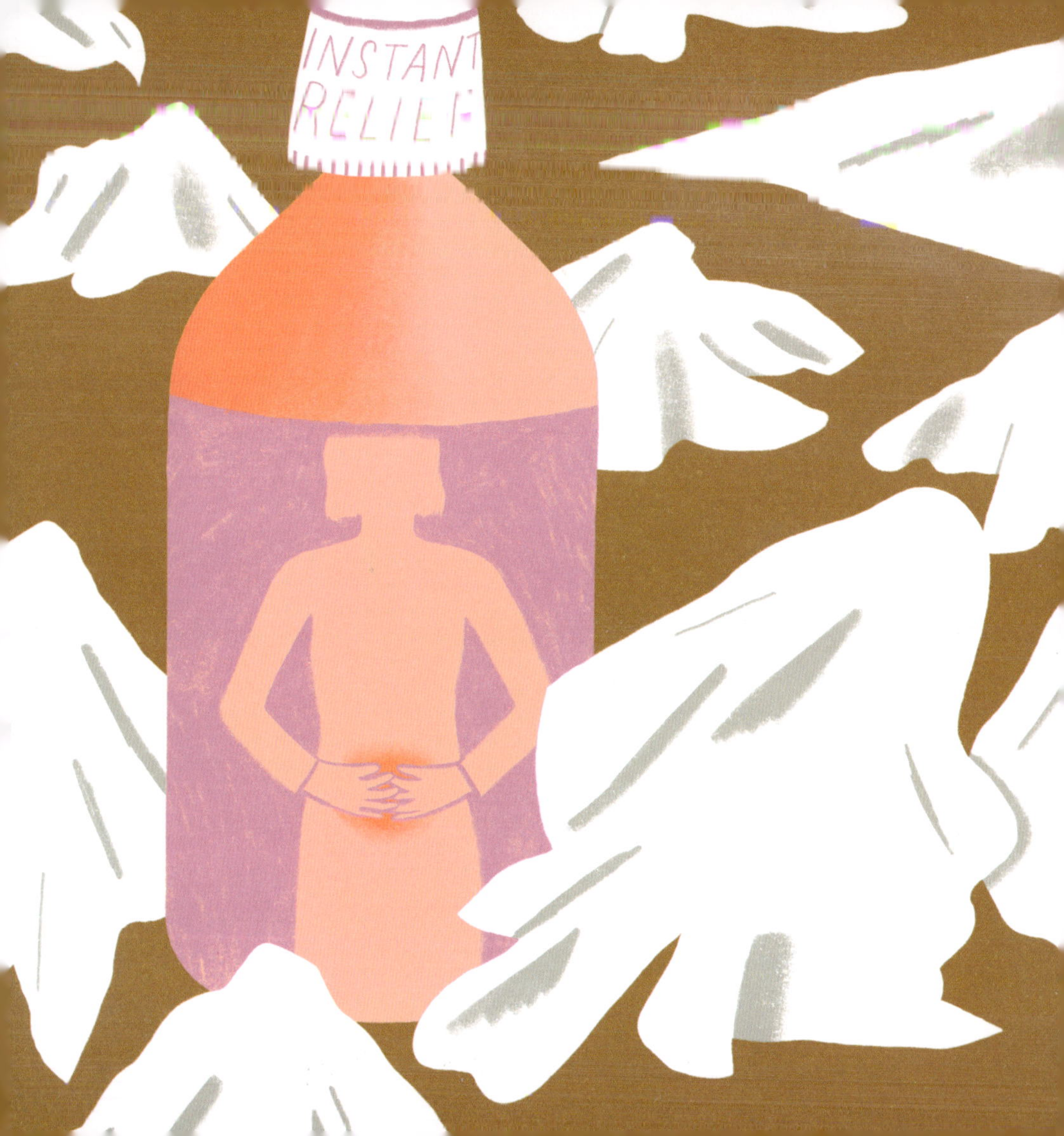
INSTANT
RELIEF

Motherhood and relaxation go together like diarrhea and sneezing.

To the Mom Sitting In the Dark,

Hey you, the mom sitting in the dark with a lump in your throat, trying to hide the heavy tears that won't stop falling. You tell yourself you don't know why, and yet you know exactly why all at the same time, it's just your feelings and thoughts are so scattered you're not sure where to start. You want to scream, want to run, want a hug, a shower, 5 goddamned minutes alone, and just 2 hours of uninterrupted sleep. Someone to listen without judgment or feeding you advice because *you've tried*, you've done everything and none of it is working. Someone to admit that this motherhood thing can be brutal and sad and frustrating while knowing that feeling those things doesn't mean you aren't also full of indescribable love, joy, and adoration for your child. You just need a moment to be off, to not be Mom; that doesn't mean that you don't want to be a mom. The worry and doubt is so loud inside of your head. You finally claw your way out of the trenches of motherhood, but when you look around, everyone else seems to know what they're doing. They're so patient and euphoric, and—just like that—you're sliding back down.

But know this: You are not alone. Not ever alone. Do not let anyone make you feel like it isn't OK to struggle. Take it one breath, one hour, one day at a time. Bad moments do not make you a bad mother. You are enough.

Love,

Your fellow mom in the dark

THE KUDOS WE ALL DESERVE

Close your eyes and move your finger over the boxes on these pages. When you feel like the time is right, stop and open your eyes to receive the kudos you deserve for something that gets taken for granted, or a message you need to read.

- You slapped together something mostly edible with whatever you could find in your kitchen like a boss.

- You stayed up to overthink for everyone like a queen.

- Do your feet hurt? 'Cause you've been running through your endless list of to-dos all day.

- You found that mystery smell like a domestic huntress vixen.

- You made those baseboards your bitch today.

- Those voices you made during story time were on point.

- You handled that unexpected blowout in the car like a badass lady MacGyver.

You thought about folding that laundry so hard, you sultry vamp!

A bad day does not make you a bad mother. Your mommy self-doubt is a Liar McLiarson and doesn't know shit.

Don't think I don't notice dat ass when you're rocking your hips in an impromptu kitchen dance party with your kids.

You did a triple threat: showered, cleaned, and cooked today!

Are you Xena? Because you wrestled that giant pile of dirty laundry like a warrior princess.

Someone is looking at you, thinking you're handling motherhood like a total boss bitch.

Who remembered to bring reusable bags into the grocery store? Suck on these totes. Captain Planet who?

Face down, ass up, that's the way you like to find past due library books under your kid's bed, like a bibliophile goddess.

You scrubbed curdled milk out of that sippy cup like a mofuckin champ.

THINGS I KNOW: WHERE EVERY SINGLE ITEM IN MY HOUSE IS; WHAT DISNEY PRINCESS I'D BE; LYRICS TO '90s R&B; USELESS MOVIE QUOTES

THINGS I DON'T KNOW: WHY I CAME INTO THIS ROOM

HOW TO MOM-PROOF YOUR HOME

Babyproofing your home is extremely important when bringing a new baby into the world. You have to lock up the cabinets, put little doohickeys over the knobs on the oven in case your newborn wants to bake a quiche, stick foam bumpers on sharp corners, and stick covers in the electrical outlets so your child won't stare at the plug's "O face," causing you to wonder if there's something wrong with them, which will then lead you to a parenting forum where you'll be chastised in the comment section by the resident Sanctimommy.

All of this is really in preparation for the padded cell you'll be headed to if you don't heed my advice. So listen up.

Put down the gazillion-piece babyproofing kit you just bought from Target and take a deep breath. Repeat after me: "I am about to mess up another human being for life. There's not enough babyproofing in the world to prevent that from happening. It's too late for my offspring, they're already brewing in my dysfunction, but there's still time to save myself."

Now that you know that there's no hope of your child escaping their adolescence unscathed by your shortcomings, you can make peace with it and move on.

Here's what you need to mom-proof your home:

→ Stock up on wine and coffee. Unlike diapers and onesies, you don't outgrow wine or caffeine. These essentials are "one size fits all."

→ Throw out all of the parenting magazines you've been furiously reading. They fill your head with delusions of grandeur and unrealistic expectations.

→ Place mirrors at every doorway of your house that leads you to the general public. Because nine times out of ten, you look like hell frozen over and then reheated. Just like your coffee.

→ Dry shampoo. Buy some. Buy all of it. Become the crazy Doomsday Prepper for gross, oily hair. Stockpile accordingly.

→ Take a break from social media. Use it only to post pictures of your adorable little cherub. The more annoying parenting advice (and friends who comment on your posts with, "When Benji was that age, he was already learning to chisel marble in the Louvre") you can part with, the better.

After becoming a mother, I really learned how to live life on the edge—of the mattress. Co-sleep, I co-sleep.

CO-SLEEPING

HOW TO CO-SLEEP IN 2,457 EASY STEPS

The term *co-sleeping* is deceiving as fuck. First there's the *co-*, meaning "jointly or mutually." I call BS. There's nothing jointly going on besides your kid's jagged toenails taking turns jabbing you in the ribs. Then there's "sleeping." Um, if by sleeping you mean 2 to 7 hours of internal screaming to an agonizing soundtrack of baby farts and your spouse's snoring, then sure, some sleeping happens.

Whether you planned on co-sleeping or gave up the good fight just to gain another glorious hour of shut-eye, there are some unspoken guidelines on how to do this thing properly.

Here's how to co-sleep in 2,457 easy steps:

1. **Visit the Grand Canyon.** Co-sleeping means you'll get a sliver of mattress allowance at the very edge of your bed, whether it's a twin or a California king. You're going to need some practice. Drive up to the Grand Canyon and spoon the edge of a sketchy-looking cliff for a night while the burro you rented donkey-kicks you in the back.

2. **Scream into your pillow.** You might not feel like you have to, but trust me, you will. Better now than at 3 a.m. when you're reenacting the "never let go" scene from *Titanic* with your shivering sanity, but on a fourth of the surface space.

3. **Play blanket tug-of-war with a boa constrictor.** Or with a tornado, or a tornado made of boa constrictors. Eighty percent of co-sleeping is struggling to keep a measly corner of your comforter to yourself while your child curls into themselves, taking the entire blanket with them into their spiral of selfishness. You will use said blanket corner wisely: 5 minutes covering one nipple, then your shoulder, then your ass cheek, etc. You'll fantasize about something horrific happening to you because at least then the first responders will give you one of those aluminum foil blanket things.

4. **Get resourceful.** Eventually, you will lose blanket tug-of-war and opt to peel the fitted sheet off the mattress and use that. Like the dirty bum that you are. Thanks a lot, family.

5. **Develop a seventh sense.** You gain a sort of seventh sense when you co-sleep that lets you know when your child is in an awkward position, or the moment your spouse even thinks about turning over. You then throw your arm across your kid and hold it there

like a pitiful meat twig barricade. If your spouse gets too close, you whack 'em. Oh, and it feels glorious. That soundly sleeping asshole deserves it anyway.

6. **Deploy flood relief.** There's no way around it. At some point, you will wake up in a warm pool of someone else's pee. But it's OK, you probably got 30 minutes of sleep, so you're golden. Like a pit crew for bedtime accidents, you change your still-slumbering child into dry, clean clothes, then lay down a couple of layers of towels, which will be just damp and scratchy enough to ensure you don't sleep for the rest of the night.

7. **My Little Poltergeist.** Your kid is going to say some weird shit in their sleep and probably wake up in a sweaty panic because they dreamed about cutting your stomach with their dinosaur toy. After writing to the Vatican because you're pretty sure your child was speaking in tongues, you'll console them like a pro, answering questions for half an hour, like "How much blood does the human body have?" and "Do you think people get cold when they're dead?" You'll then spend the rest of the night staring at your child in wide-eyed dismay. Good luck getting any sleep. Not with Beelzebub incarnate occupying your bed.

8. **Surrender self-defense.** I don't know what kids dream about, but I'm pretty sure it's similar to WWE's *SmackDown Live*. You will be beaten to within an inch of your life, and, because you're a mom, you'll let it slide just so your child can get their recommended 13 hours of sleep.

9.------2,457. **Attempt Kama Sleep-tra.** Kids transition through an awkward progression of sleep positions, forcing you to come up with your own counter-sleep positions. Like a shitty game of bed Tetris where you lose no matter what.

Can't wait until bedtime so I can get in at least 6 hours of mom guilt, worrying, and brainstorming of witty comebacks to completely made-up conflicts. Like a random "mompreneur" trying to sell me on weight-loss wraps 1 week after having a baby.

MARRY, SCREW, KILL FOR PARENTS

Down for some saucy fun? Below you'll find groups of three fictional characters that you must opt to either marry, have sex with, or kill *without* doing the same action with more than one prospect. Sound easy? Give it a shot!

Caillou's Dad, Daddy Pig, or Inspector Gadget?

Robbie Rotten, Shawn Hunter, or Bud Bundy?

Zack Morris, Kevin Arnold, or Jonathan Taylor Thomas?

Red Forman, Al Bundy, or Tim "The Tool Man" Taylor?

Winnie Cooper, Slater, or Devon Sawa (i.e., Casper the Ghost as a human)?

Topanga, Kelly Kapowski, or Will Smith as the Fresh Prince of Bel-Air?

Steve Urkel, Steve from the original *Blue's Clues*, or Screech?

Mr. Bean, Pee-Wee Herman, or Carlton Banks?

Mister Rogers, LeVar Burton, or Bill Nye the Science Guy?

All of the Power Rangers, all of the Wiggles, or all of the Teletubbies?

Fred Flintstone, George Jetson, or Shaggy?

Goofy, Scooby Doo, or Snoopy?

John Smith, the Beast, or Tarzan?

Robin Hood the fox, Tod from *The Fox and the Hound*, or Nick Wilde from *Zootopia*?

Wreck-It Ralph, Maui, or Megamind?

Flynn Rider, Prince Eric, or Peter Pan?

Doogie Howser, Cory Matthews, or Fez?

Jafar, Hades, or Shan Yu?

Gaston, Hercules, or Kocoum?

Animal, Alf, or Sulley?

Mr. Tanner, Principal Belding, or Uncle Phil?

Li Shang, Kristoff, or Prince Naveen from *The Princess and the Frog*?

FOUR SCORE AND SEVEN YEARS AGO...

Me telling a single, childless person about th. last time I was cool and a hoe

If you're a parent who has never gotten irrationally angry about someone wiggling their toes while sitting next to you, how's it feel to be a fucking liar?

FIVE YOGA POSES FOR DEALING WITH YOUR CHILD'S BULLSHIT

Yoga isn't usually my thing, but there are times as a mother when I could really use some inner chill. Give me a soft mat and an hour or so to be in the horizontal position, meditating on the back of my eyelids. Here are five yoga poses for different situations you may find yourself in. Motherhood is fun. Hopefully you can find some zen instead of rage-screaming into a pillow.

DOWNWARD ASSHOLE

You made a rookie move and forgot to watch your step. Now your foot is throbbing, thanks to a Lego land mine. Stop dead in your tracks and take a deep breath of regret and hatred for an inanimate object. Allow each curse word to pass through your clenched teeth in a tense hiss as your child watches. Bend over while bringing the affected foot to your hands. Stand there fuming. And release.

MOTHER'S POSE

Oh no. You're in public, and your child just curled into an immovable ball of outrage.

To diffuse a Rebellious Child's Pose, you must counter it with Mother's Pose. Stepping forward with one foot, allow your other knee to drop, placing you in a deep lunge. Imagine that your arms are a straitjacket, extend them in front of you, and grab your little tantrum-throwing a-hole. Give him a little squeeze, so he knows you mean business. This pose transitions into resistance training, as you speed-walk out of the store with a flailing pile of limbs under your arm like an angry football.

BEDTIME SALUTATIONS

You've just put your child to bed and successfully exited their room, dodging requests for more story time. As soon as you are out of eyesight, widen your stance. Now do a deep squat while simultaneously crossing your arms in front of you. Spring up into the standing position and spread your arms out wide. Now do a twirl like Maria from *The Sound of Music* and march over to the couch to binge-watch some much-deserved trash TV.

DOWNWARD SPIRAL

Your limit has been reached. Your fucks quota for the day is maxed out, but your more-than-capable-of-doing-so-themself child is hollering at you from the bathroom to wipe their butt. Suddenly, the floor is beginning to rise. Just let it happen. Now that you're literally at your lowest point of the day, lie on your back and bring both your legs up into the air. Now just start helicoptering your legs around as you beat the ground with your fists. Toss your head from side to side. Go ahead and crumble to the ground. Thrash around until the third holler.

USTRESSMAMA

Oh, neat. You're driving on a busy road, and your child has dropped something he's deemed vital to his existence. He is now in the back seat signaling the coming of the apocalypse with pterodactyl-like shrieks.

While keeping your eyes on the road, and one hand on the steering wheel, you need to contort your body and lean as far back as you can. Reach your free arm behind your seat, and blindly swat around like a complete asshole. This is remarkably like fishing. You will grab things from the back seat that you thought were gone forever. Ideally, you'll find the object your child dropped. Possibly more than ideally, you'll find a toy that the aforementioned tyrant dropped on a previous excursion, and it will pacify him until you are able to stop and get out of your car.

B'ADAWANNA

Your child is hungry. They have requested a PB&J. You made the requested PB&J, and even cut it into triangles, as per your child's specifications, but in the time it took you to set the sandwich on a plate and turn around to serve it, your child has decided they want something else.

They start whining, and this is the pinnacle of shit you do not want to deal with today. Time for B'adawanna. First, drop to your knees. Second, lose control of every muscle in your body and free-fall face-first onto the ground. You're so fed up that you don't even shield your face as you go down. Is it bedtime yet?

RAP NAMES FOR KIDS

My kid: Can you hold this?

Me (Hanging one-handed from a cliff, seconds away from death): .....

TACTICAL HAND SIGNALS FOR PARENTS

The kids are finally asleep. Score.

Stop. I can't even right now.

It smells like it's your turn to change the diaper.

How does that even happen?

Let's play the game where you don't talk anymore.

I don't... I'm not even sure how to clean up this many fluids.

Hang on. Does this story have a point or an ending?

Gooooo in time-out. Go there.

Fill my glass up with this much wine.

Why is it so quiet?
Looks like a little a-hole. This tall.
I. AM. watching. You.
Rolling up my sleeves to catch the "mud trout" in the tub.
Do I look like an idiot?
I can't unsee this.
What. Is. This?
Clean. It. Up. Now.
Watch your tone.

To the Mom I Wanted to Be,

We thought we had it all figured out, didn't we? We added only the very best of everything to our baby registry, pinned healthy lunch ideas to carefully curated Pinterest boards, and pored over baby books by parenting experts who doled out one-size-fits-all advice. We listened to the horror stories of seasoned parents while smugly saying to ourselves, *My kid will never act like that.*

The first time I felt you slipping away was the second night at home with our baby. I was a mix of frazzle and frenzy all at once because he wouldn't sleep. He just cried. Surely, I'd already screwed up the first steps to that successful bedtime routine I memorized from the parenting magazine. "His days and nights are switched," someone said. "You're spoiling him by letting him sleep on you," rambled another. And I realized then: I have to say goodbye to you.

I assembled you methodically from what I read and saw, from people I admired. You were pretty amazing: fun and energetic, hands-on and tough. You served healthy foods, limited screen time, and you didn't let the bad days get to you. You're the fun mom all the neighborhood kids talk about. You don't wear yoga pants or leave the house without applying makeup. You shower and exercise and, and, and. . . you started to kill me.

You were getting too big, too demanding. The lesson plans, activities, and need to have it all were devouring me. Every perceived failure, every time we fell short of a milestone. Every time my child refused to even lick one of those broccoli tots some stranger online convinced me would taste *just like potatoes*, you were there tapping your foot at me. *Tsk tsk tsk*. Every time I blindly picked my outfit out from dirty clothes strewn across the floor at 4 a.m., or let the TV babysit my child so I could cook a meal or take a shower or eat a candy bar without sharing, you were there haunting me.

And it's OK. I'm OK. I am enough without you. You, reading this—you are enough.

I can't choose what type of mother to be because we don't get to choose what kind of child we *get*. But don't worry about the kids, OK? Turns out they're pretty great regardless of what I wear as long as I just show up every day. My "doing the best I can" is what's best for them. They may live solely on a diet of chicken nuggets and mac 'n' cheese, but at least they're fed and happy.

Sometimes the best thing to do is to cut ties with the mom you thought you'd be, the fantasy life you hold on to so tightly inside your head, and fall in love with the mom you've grown into—perfectly imperfect, but trying her damndest.

Love,

The Mom I Turned Out to Be

I might not be great at keeping the house clean, cooking, showering, wearing actual pants, or being a super mom, but am I great at staying fit, time management, constantly entertaining my children, maintaining friendships, and achieving my goals? Also no.

WHAT KIND OF MOM ARE YOU?

YOU LIKE TO GO ON LONG WALKS AT:

A. The craft store.

B. Colleges your three-year-old may attend one day.

C. Walk? You'd rather paddle, longboard, or rollerskate with your derby team, Mombie Mayhem.

D. The liquor store.

IT'S SPIRIT WEEK AT YOUR CHILD'S SCHOOL. YOU:

A. Bask in the delighted smiles of your kids as they head into school oozing the day's theme from head to toe. After school you're taking them to the trampoline park.

B. Hire a photographer to do a photo shoot of the outfits you've been planning since Spirit Week last year so you can upload them to your blog.

C. Rallied and made outfits and accessories with your mom BFFs while drinking margaritas until 1 a.m.. Your kids look awesome and will be the talk of the school.

D. Yell, "Yay, school spirit!" as you turn down the music you're blasting and come to a rolling stop so that your kids can jump out of the car.

WHAT'S IN YOUR DIAPER BAG/PURSE?

A. Bento box filled with yummy, healthy snacks, baby essentials, your kid's favorite toys, items they'll need for all their scheduled activities for the day, and the current read from your Mom and Tot book club.

B. Sunscreen, protein bars, fruit infuser water bottles, emergency contact cards, changes of clothes, sanitizing wipes, tissues, a first aid kit, essential oils . . .

C. Concert tickets, lipstick, snack, tablet, and point-and-shoot camera.

D. Diaper bag? You use a plastic bag or a Crown Royal sack.

HOW ARE YOU WEARING YOUR HAIR?

A. Half up, half down in modified fishtail braids. Just like you saw you favorite celeb mom wearing hers yesterday.

B. Beachy waves. Or in a cute, high pony on Mondays, Wednesdays, and Thursdays from 9 a.m. to 3:30 p.m. when you help out in your kid's class as Room Mom.

C. A cute messy bun with freshly cut bangs and a little bit of dry shampoo sprayed in because you were up late last night at a karaoke bar with friends.

D. The way you woke up with it, plus probably a few more crumbs and bodily fluids.

YOUR KID'S BEDTIME ROUTINE ENTAILS:

A. Board games, cookie decorating, pillow fights, learning about the stars through their new telescope, heartfelt conversation about their day, funny stories you make up for them, lights out after exactly ten hugs and kisses.

B. Bath, teeth brushed, and two stories. All done while you speak Japanese to help with language immersion.

C. Nightly kitchen dance party, meditating, showers, and 30 minutes of audiobooks while you get in some snuggle time.

D. Yelling at the kids over your favorite show to hit the sack so mommy can drink her special juice and enjoy some effing silence.

WHEN YOUR CHILD HAS A FIELD TRIP, YOU:

A. Drop them off blasting Jay-Z after waking up early to grab a pancake breakfast at your favorite restaurant.

B. Chaperone and bring homemade, organic, allergy-free snacks to enjoy on the bus you've decorated to go along with the trip theme. You've also designed cutesy pop-up itineraries.

C. Decide to play hooky and go explore the art district before checking out the concert at the skate park, which you'll watch while enjoying a smorgasbord of food truck eats.

D. OH SHIT, WHAT TRIP? WHAT CHILD? WHAT DAY IS IT!?

ANSWERS

MOSTLY A'S: Super Mom! How? How are you so bloody amazing? You are the holy grail of motherdom—fun, hip, organized, positive, crafty—the list goes on and on, and you make it all look effortless. Seriously, can you adopt us? Because we want in on the fun!

MOSTLY B'S: Put-Together Mom. You plan things out ahead of time, are prepared for any scenario, always on time, and always looking your best. Your home is well-kept, but what's more impressive is that your car is clean! No one knows how the hell you're able to manage everything like such a baddie, and we're all fucking jealous.

MOSTLY C'S: C for Cool Mom. Yup, you're the unicorn mama all the other moms secretly want to be. You somehow balance being a mom, having a social life, and your unique identity like a total badass. You don't try too hard, and you're never pretending to be something you're not—which is why you're so fucking cool!

MOSTLY D'S: Hot Mess Mom. You tell it how it is, and while it might sound harsh, hot mess moms are a good time and make for some of the best friends. You don't put on airs, and you don't judge because you know the struggle is real. Also, a staple of your mom uniform is leggings—so that if anyone crosses you or your babies, you're ready and able to deliver roundhouse kicks that jeans wouldn't allow for.

THE REAL ANSWER: You're all of these. Every mom is. Sure, some of us weigh heavier in one or more personality categories, but it usually just depends on the time, the day, emotions, how much sleep we got, and how much dumbfuckery we've had to withstand lately. So, as you're skimming the other answers, maybe wishing you scored differently, know that you're perfect just the way you are. The you that you are is the mom your kid needs.

Damn, it feels good to be a gangster
—Me while starting a load of laundry without even separating the whites, colors, and towels

I made food for my kid, set it down in front of them like they were going to eat it, and then we just laughed and laughed.

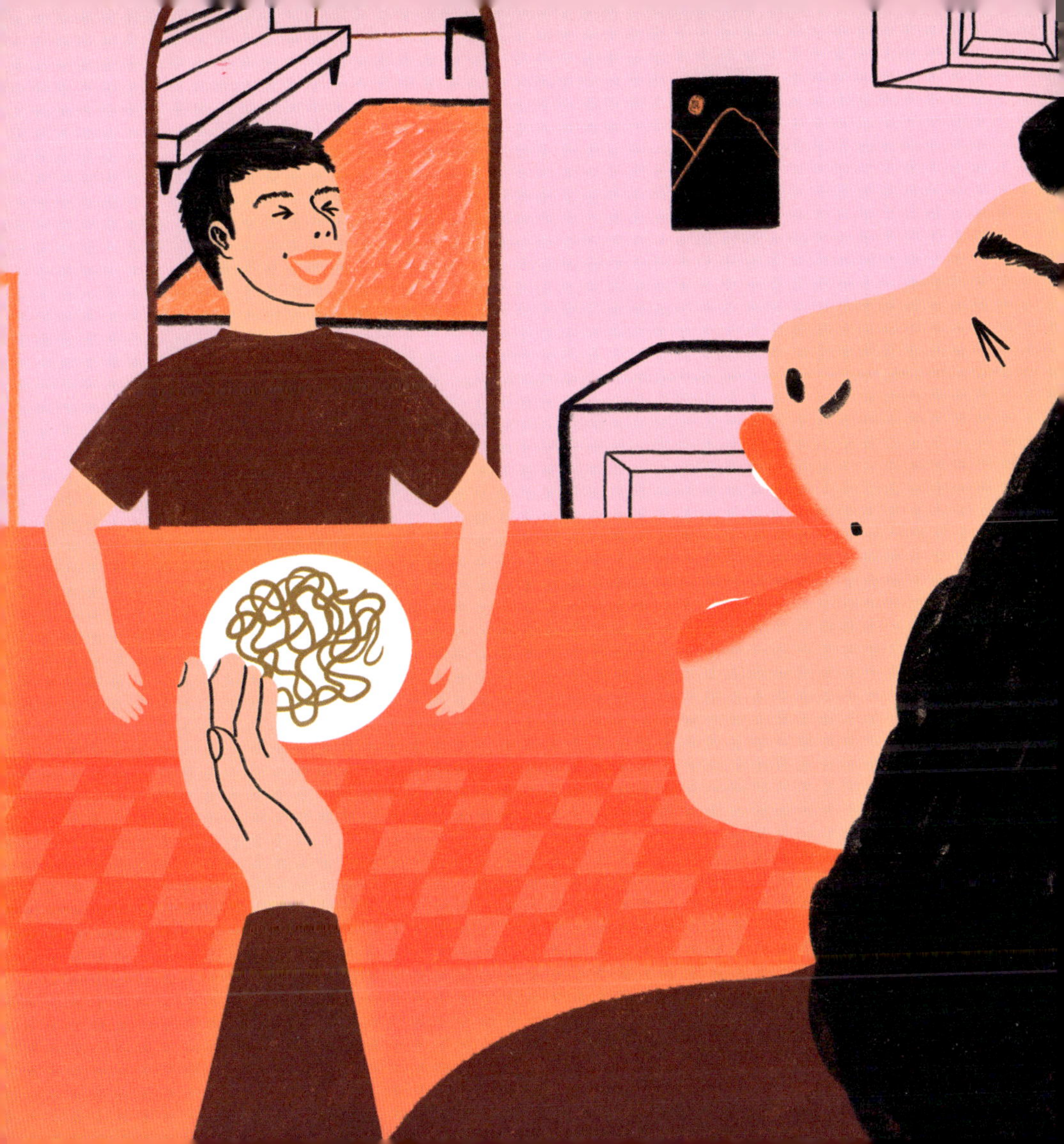

SEX POSITIONS FOR PARENTS

FROZEN

You're about to "let it go," but one of your kids busts through your door, so you and your partner just lie there, frozen, pretending to be asleep on top of each other.

NETFLIX & CHILL

Where he says he wants to see you in control. Of the remote. And you scroll Netflix so hard while enjoying each other's company from opposite ends of the couch.

MR. CLEAN

Where he puts his oversize load in your hot, wet box and treats your filthy stains with top-notch detergent and fabric softener. Then, just as you're coming down from your spin cycle, he pulls out and immediately . . . puts all the laundry into the dryer. I don't know about you, but my chime setting just went from quiet to loud.

LUCY & DESI

Where you do it '50s style and have a foursome with you, your significant other, and your separate beds.

PHONE SECS

That thing your spouse does that drives you wild where they call to say they're gonna be home in just a second to help put the kids to bed. Oh, and they ordered pizza for dinner.

BEDTIME IS WHERE REPEATEDLY SAYING "GOODNIGHT" TO YOUR KIDS PROGRESSES FROM A SWEET WHISPER TO A DEATH METAL ROAR

TACTICS FOR EXITING A SLEEPING CHILD'S ROOM

Before reading any further, go ahead and grab a can of WD-40 and grease the hinges of every door in every room in your entire house. This is serious business right here, and we don't take chances. It's time to case the joint.

Once you've covered your bases, you can practice the art of exiting a sleeping child's room.

Crouching Asshole, Sleeping Baby

Listen, it's OK. You're an asshole, I'm an asshole. We all do asshole things for our asshole kids, and naptime is no different.

The moment your baby has closed their eyes, you need to slowly lower yourself into the crouching position. It is imperative that you remove yourself from their line of sight.

Once on the ground, crawl to the nearest exit at a snail's pace. Children have superhuman hearing and can hear your legs sliding through the carpet much like a gazelle can sense a lion preparing to pounce from tall grass.

Red Light, Green Light

Yup, not just a kid's game! Kids are shit at judging distance, which is why they are always either directly in your face or 5 miles farther away than you told them they could go. Use this to your advantage.

As long as you're still in the room each time they open their eyes those first 10 minutes to 2 hours, then their trust has been earned and they will zonk out.

When you lay your kid down, sit down on the floor. Each time they aren't paying attention or close their eyes, scooch yourself a little bit closer to the door until they're asleep.

Remember to stretch before attempting either of these exit strategies. Even the most brilliant exit plan can be foiled by the cracking noises of your decrepit, aging bones.

I bet I can guess what you are with just one question.
Do you have kids? Then: tired. You're fucking tired.

If you thought your WTFs couldn't get any WTF-ier, try having kids.

THINGS PARENTS CAN ADD TO THEIR RÉSUMÉ

Parenthood is a tough gig, but you also acquire a very particular set of skills. Skills you have learned over many sleepless nights and tantrums. Skills that translate into occupations you are qualified for only once you become a parent:

- Professional Chimpanzee Wrangler
- Angry, Flailing Octopus Shoe Putter-Onner
- Secret Vegetable Smuggler
- Hulk Calmer-Downer
- Patient Injury Kisser
- Master Evil-Eye Giver
- "How to Survive the Zombie Apocalypse with the Contents of Your Diaper Bag" Instructor
- Expert Item Locator
- Professional Question Taker
- Bathtub Poop Fisherman

The possibilities!

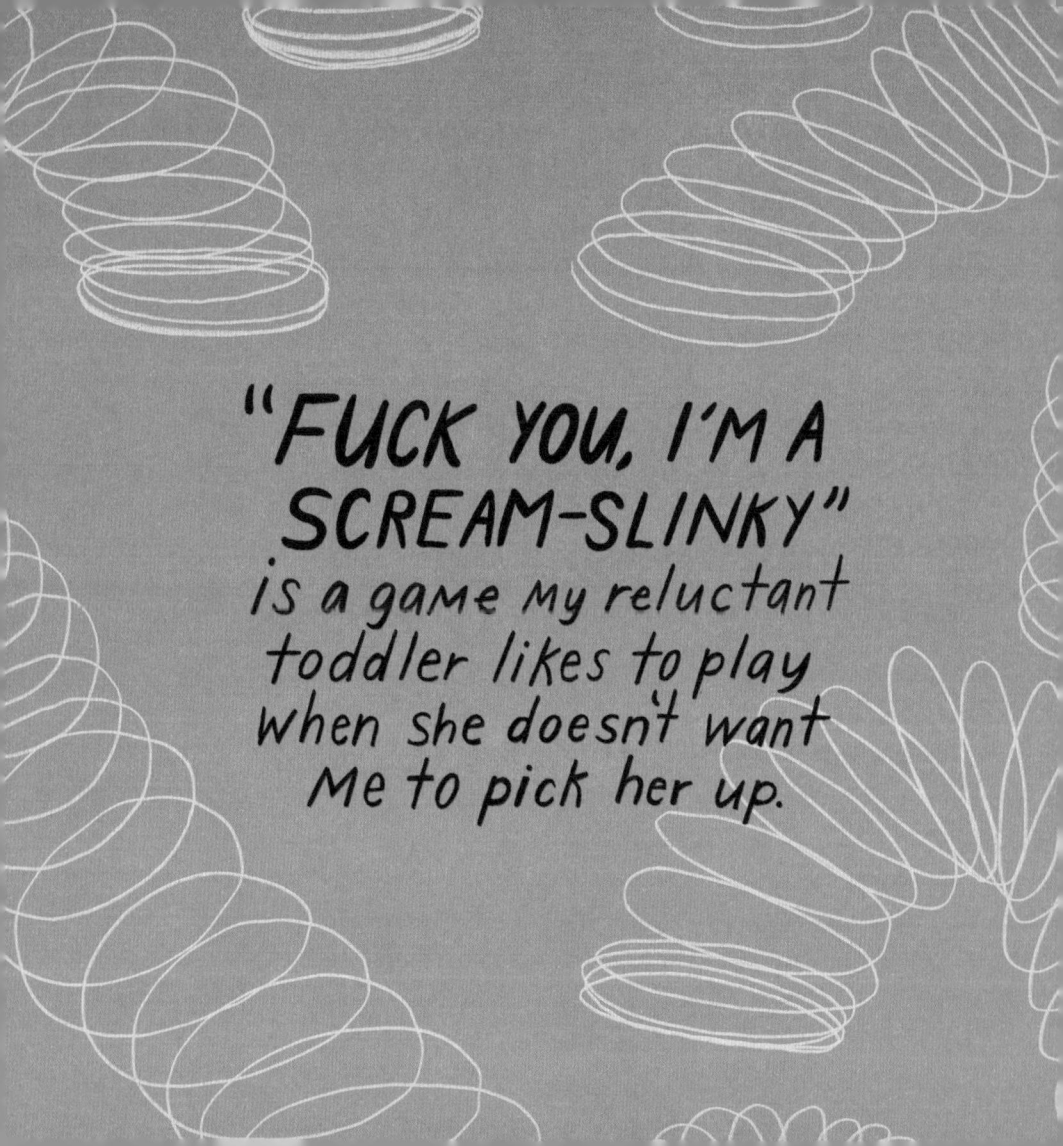

"FUCK YOU, I'M A SCREAM-SLINKY" is a game my reluctant toddler likes to play when she doesn't want me to pick her up.

A TIMELINE OF GOING ANYWHERE WITH KIDS

Getting kids ready to go anywhere should be a torture method practiced by CIA agents. "Oh, you don't want to tell us who you work for? Well, here's a four-year-old. Persuade him to put his socks and shoes on within 10 minutes, and you're free to walk."

It just ain't gonna happen.

Prepping children to leave the house is like experiencing a mental breakdown in slo-mo. Why? Because children are constantly looking for ways to rebel. They are tiny parasites who feed on your rage and sorrow. They also have short attention spans and live in a world of wonder wherein infinite possibilities exist.

HERE'S A REALISTIC TIMELINE FOR GETTING KIDS READY TO GO SOMEWHERE:

1 hour until estimated time of departure (ETD):

Parent experiences memory loss, probably due to sustained head injuries from being bludgeoned with a plastic dinosaur. They are unable to recollect past attempts at leaving the house on time and, as a result, think they have plenty of time to get out the door.

30 minutes until ETD:

Parent begins to get themself ready, but gets repeatedly bombarded by multiple rounds of Twenty Questions. Children become very inquisitive about their parent's appearance and outfit choices, and can be heard asking things like, "Why do your underwear go inside of your butt like that?" followed by maniacal giggling.

20 minutes until ETD:

Parent notes that they've forgotten to feed their kid, and arrive at the decision that they really don't want to deal with a hangry monster while in the public eye.

18 minutes until ETD:
Parent frantically strips their child of all clothing after they managed to spill and smear the majority of their food and drink all over themself.

10 minutes until ETD:
Parent tells their child to use the restroom and to put on their socks and shoes, while they go on a mad dash around the house to pack a bag of essentials.

2 minutes past ETD:
Parent screams at their kid to put all their clothes back on and stop using their shoes as hand puppets, and mutters a string of profanities as they continue the search for their child's favorite toy.

20 minutes past ETD:
After finally getting your child buckled into their car seat (see pages 88–89 for how that plays out) and driving down the street, parent realizes they've left their phone and bag at home.

HOW TO (NOT) GET YOUR CHILD INTO A CAR SEAT

Few tasks yield more resistance and mindfuckery from your child than getting them into their car seat.

It all sounds so simple: Pick up your kid, set them down in their car seat, adjust and secure the car seat straps, and drive off into the sunset. Unfortunately, babies are born into this world with car-seat-repellent limbs.

Straight from the shitty parent's instruction manual, here's how to (not) get your kid into a car seat.

1. TAKE THEM TO THE CAR.

Getting kids to go, or do, anything when you want them to is a rare and laughable feat. You can deploy every parenting tactic you have. Children do not give a decimal of a shit. Prepare for screaming, wiggling, thrashing, and did I mention screaming?

2. PICK UP YOUR SPAWN.

The moment the thought "car seat" enters your mind, your child will sense it like a predator smelling fear, and they will enter sack-of-potatoes mode. This is where they decide to lose all control of their body, resulting in a sort of full-body emergency break via dead weight.

3. PLACE YOUR CHILD IN THEIR CAR SEAT.

Limbs will be flailing and grabbing onto things for dear life, and your kid will be slippery from all of the crying. You will lean in close and whisper threats, only to turn around and realize the entire neighborhood or parking lot is staring at you. Oh, because you're all so fucking PERFECT, right?

4. ADJUST AND SECURE ALL OF THE STRAPS.

Good luck, that's all I have to say. By now, your offspring will be utilizing every move in their "fuck you" arsenal to stop or delay what is happening. To cooperate would mean to give up what little control they have in their lives, and they will not go gentle into that good night. The moment you get one limb secured and move on to the next, they've slipped out of their restraints. Like whack-a-mole, but ten times more infuriating.

5. GIVE UP.

Cancel your plans, because life is not happening today. Jesus take the wheel. Neighbors be damned. After you finish putting the diaper bag away and check in on the Possessed, you discover that your child is now fast asleep. Great.

SORRY I'M LATE (A TARDY SLIP FOR PARENTS)

My kid:

- Had a blowout.
- Wanted to buckle their own seat belt/car seat.
- Was mad about (circle all that apply): a bump in their sock/their toenail getting snagged on their sock/their shirt being too itchy/a tag on their clothing.
- Wanted to (circle all that apply): zip up their own jacket/put on their own shoes/put on their own socks/dress themself/bring all their favorite toys.
- Was throwing an epic tantrum.
- Threw up in the car.

I:

- Forgot.
- Had to wrestle my child into their car seat.
- Was debating whether or not our friendship warranted pants and a bra. Before you get offended, I'm here, aren't I?
- Was rage-wrapping your child's gift in the driveway/parking lot.
- Was having a mental breakdown in my car.
- Needed to pick up coffee despite running late because I need it to function and not slap everyone.
- Had to pick up food on the way because my kid claimed to be starving even though I fed them right before I left (which is also the reason I'm late).
- Didn't want to come.

When I'm old, as payback I'm gonna giggle uncontrollably, squirm, and go all sack-of-potatoes on my son when he tries to get me in the car.

HOW TO CALM YOUR TITS

Kids are hard, there's no denying it. Learn how to cope with their shenanigans before you earn yourself a bed in the mental institution. Even though most days that sounds like a spa day.

> **Meditate.** Meditate on the backs of your eyelids the next time your kids are waging war on your nerves.

> **Exercise.** Go into an empty room, throw yourself on the floor, and start flailing. Bang your fists against the carpet. No, sweetie, Mommy's not having a mental breakdown, this is exercise.

> **Drink a glass of wine.** It's five o'clock somewhere, and you're a mom. Enough said.

Eat a healthy snack. Like an entire cake.

Jam out with your clam out. Put on some gangsta rap and have a dance sesh in your kitchen.

Drink another glass of wine. *Chug! Chug! Chug! Chug!*

Have a laugh. Just try it. Giggle a little bit. Now giggle about giggling at nothing. Do it louder. Louder so that your kids can hear you. Start flailing around. Let your kids see just how batshit crazy you can be. Plant the seed of fear into them—fear that Mommy is unstable.

I'd like us all to take a moment of silence. I don't have a reason; I'd just really appreciate some silence in this house right now.

MOTHERHOOD IS PUTTING THE SAME SEVEN OBJECTS AWAY THIRTY TIMES A DAY

11 RULES FOR PLAYDATING MY CHILD

There's an unspoken etiquette among parents that I thought I'd shed light on. Because, while most of these should just be common sense, it's something I've found not everyone possesses.

1. Go ahead and factor in a 30-minute delay when we make plans. Shit happens. Sometimes said shit is literal shit.

2. Thou shalt not say a farking thing if you notice me wearing the same thing 2 (or 3, or 4) days in a row.

3. Come bearing alcohol or coffee.

4. Tell me if your kid is sick before our playdate.

5. "Come as you are." Bring me your tired, your reeking, your frazzled, your frumpy.

6. Thou shalt compliment my home even if it resembles a truck stop bathroom after Penny Hot Dog Night at the Shityourself Festival, which is known for serving up a complimentary side of food poisoning.

7. Your snacks are my snacks; my snacks are your snacks.

8. Do not utter the words "I would never let my child do that" or "My child would never do that" in my presence.

9. A morning-of "Are we still doing a playdate?" text is obligatory. When you have kids, plans change at least every half hour.

10. She who initiates conversation of a playdate shall host said playdate. Don't be trying to pawn your kids off for a free night of babysitting so you can go enjoy $2 Margarita Night.

11. If other parents are involved, I need names and a brief summary on their level of uppityness. I need to know if I have to put on actual pants or not.

MAGIC 8-BALL FOR MOMS

To use this Magic 8-Ball:

1. Ask a question like "Is that mystery smell I can't seem to find me?" or "Should I get 'always tired' tattooed on my face like Post Malone so my family will hopefully get the hint?
2. Close your eyes.
3. Tap your finger on this page in random locations 8 times.
4. On your eighth tap, open your eyes to discover your answer.

- GET IT!
- LOL
- NOPE NOPE NOPE
- NO, BECAUSE KIDS
- IDK!
- YASS!
- FUCK YES!
- WHY NOT?
- YEAH RIGHT
- NOT UNTIL THE KIDS ARE MOVED OUT
- I THINK A DRINK WILL HELP
- NEVER AGAIN
- ALL OF THE NOPES
- YOU GOT THIS!
- MEH
- YOLO!

They should make a movie with Disney princesses as moms, where they sing about wanting uninterrupted sleep, a shower, and not to be anyone's snack bitch for just one day.

HOW TO CLEAN THE BATHROOM WHEN YOU'RE A BOY MOM:

1. DOUSE THE TOILET WITH GASOLINE.

2. LIGHT IT ON FIRE.

WHEN KIDS CRY: VERY SCIENCEY STATISTICS

Tantrums are the leading cause of alcohol consumption in parents.

100% of the world's children cry just to bring dishonor on their family.

100% of the world's parents are dead on the inside as a result.

Peak times for crying:

Out in public

When you're on the phone

Leaving literally anywhere

Bedtime

Hours ending in a.m. or p.m.

What kids use to dry their snot and tears

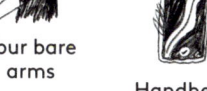

- Your bare arms
- Handheld electronics
- The couch cushions
- Your dog
- Important paperwork
- Your hair

Things you try to calm them the fuck down

- Sugary delights
- Glorious screen time
- Getting loud
- Making a giant ass of yourself

Typical success rate of these tactics: **0%**

HOW TO PEE IF YOU'RE A BOY

If you're a boy mom, you know that once you start potty-training, your bathrooms will look and smell like a thing of nightmares.

Going number one when you're a little boy can be tricky, so I've slapped together this fun little how-to guide. Feel free to add more disgusting pee acts or modify the steps as you see fit.

1. Begin by pissing all over the seat. Be liberal. Be thorough. Lift the toilet seat up and pee all over the bottom of it, paying special attention to the little screws at the hinges that hold it in place, and on top of the toilet rim. Don't be a slacker. Outline the impossible-to-clean crevices of the toilet's base like a disgusting tinkle goblin.

2. Because you have a bottomless bladder, you are the Neverending Story of pungent piss, usually at the most inconvenient times and places, like in the pot of an artificial ficus tree in the middle of a funeral service.

3. Now it's time to get rid of any excess by shaking it "like a Polaroid picture." Be sure to step away from the toilet during this time so that you leave a trail of pee droplets on the bathroom floor for Mommy to step in later (Hansel and Gretel style).

4. Before you leave the bathroom, you need to ensure that the pee you've gotten on your hands dries into a thin, slightly tacky film. Stall a little bit. Make faces in the mirror, paint the mirror with your tongue, use Mommy's toothbrush like a screwdriver to pretend-loosen those urine-soaked screws on the toilet lid, and touch every surface possible with your gross hands.

5. Now that the pee film on your hands has been baked to perfection, exit the bathroom. No need to actually wash your hands and flush the toilet; that's a fun little gift you like to leave for Mommy to find later. She loves it. Now go up to your mother and affectionately grab her by the face with both of your pee hands. Play that game where you mess with her lips while she makes noise—*Brrrrbrrrrbrrr*—or pretend to be a dentist and use your fingers to give Mom an exam.

FOR FUCK'S SAKE!

MY RESPONSE TO EVERYTHING AS A MOM

Let's play a game called How Many Times Will Mommy Repeat Herself Before She Loses Her Shit?

AM I A GOOD PARENT? QUIZ

LET'S HASH THIS WHOLE THING OUT ONCE AND FOR ALL WITH A QUIZ.

1. Did food, or something loosely resembling food, enter your child's scream hole?

2. Was aforementioned food mostly clean?

3. Did your child receive a bath this week, or come into contact with water, such as via swimming, the sprinkler, spilling water on themself, or you blasting them with the hose or sink sprayer after discovering that they'd eaten all your chocolate?

4. Does your child know that you (mostly) love them?

5. Did you listen to your child for at least 5 minutes total in the past 48 hours?

6. Did they whine because you wouldn't let them do or have something in the last 24 hours?

7. Did they emit a noise that resembled laughter today?

8. Do you look like a steaming pile of garbage right now?

9. Did you talk to, or attempt a form of communication, such as grunting, with your child?

10. Does your child have somewhere to sleep? (A drawer counts.)

11. Did you try to brush your child's teeth this week?

12. Does your house look like a tornado hurled the contents of Toys "R" Us and the dollar store all over your home?

13. Did your child drink something nonpoisonous today? (Bathwater counts.)

IF YOU'VE ANSWERED YES TO THREE OR MORE OF THESE QUESTIONS, CONGRATULATIONS! YOU'RE A GOOD PARENT.

I'm going to start explaining my age the way we do for dogs. Like, yeah, I'm in my thirties but in mom years, I'm more like seventy-four.

Less "my kid would never do that!" and more peekaboo with kids in shopping carts while their frazzled moms aren't looking. That's how you build the village.

AFTERWORD

If you're a mom, I might not know you, but I've cleaned up the same diapers, cried myself to sleep over the same mom guilt, felt like I was failing at the same things, questioned if I could wear my favorite shirt another day without washing it and decided that absolutely I could, scream-whispered at my kid in the grocery store, and been determined to be a super mom all day only to end up crying along with my child. JUST. LIKE. YOU. Not a single one of us has an iota of a clue as to what we're doing, so if I see you in the store, frazzled or trying to laugh off something awkward or TMI that your kid told a stranger, and I give you a smile—know that in that smile, I'm saying I understand, I've been there, I *am* there, and I'm right here, sitting in the shit with you.

The mom with a fresh blowout (that isn't of the poosplosion variety) and full face of makeup you saw at the store? She treated herself for the first time in 2 years. She normally can only get a shower in twice a year, like in fucking medieval times. The mom with the three well-behaved kids at the park while your one and only is throwing an epic tantrum in the middle of the rope bridge? She's been losing her goddamned mind all day and had to get out of the house to save what's left of her sanity. Maybe if she tires out her kids she can Al Bundy it up, spread-eagle on the couch with one hand down her pants, remote in the other, happily scrolling for some trash TV to watch. The mom who posts all the crafts and activities she does with her child while you feel guilty about letting yours binge on screen time? She feels like she's lost herself in motherhood, and art reminds her of who she was before all this. The mom with the amazing career? She sometimes feels guilty about not being a stay-at-home mom and is sick of the double standard that because she's a woman she should give up her profession. The SAHM? She misses her job but didn't make enough after paying childcare to keep it. She loves watching all the milestones happen but would give anything to be off duty from snack bitching for a bit.

We're all super mom. We're all hot mess mom. We're all cool mom, frazzled mom, tired mom, boss bitch mom, put-together mom, fun mom, and struggling mom. And we're all in this together through the not-so-#Blessed moments and the moments that feel like we're riding a flaming dumpster downhill into a major interstate.

ACKNOWLEDGMENTS

Thank you (and I'm sorry) to my son and daughter, who inspired all of this malarkey and taught me how to be a mother. Thank you to my husband for loving me when I don't feel lovable. Thank you to my old sea dog and author of a father who taught me how to curse and write. Thank you to my mom—I love you. I get it now. Thank you to my amazing funny internet friends (BBZ, Illuminatrixes, Family Bed, and Bats) for your support, encouragement, inspiration, and most of all—helping me not feel so alone. Thank you to my family and friends, and thank you to Chronicle and my editors for believing in me and letting me speak on parenting in a (very explicit) voice that I think is so important for people to hear. Lastly, thank you to anyone reading this—you are so much more amazing than you realize or get credit for.